HOW TO DRAW

FUN, FAB FACES

FUN FOR AGES 6-106

A FUN, STEP-BY-STEP GUIDE TO DRAWING AND COLORING FEMALE FACES

KAREN CAMPBELL

About this book

I spent the last 5 years teaching kids how to paint and draw everything from fashion figures to monster trucks. This book is for my students. My hope is that this book can reach more students than I ever thought possible. Thank you for believing in art and believing in me. I believe in you.

Author, Illustrator, Publisher: Karen Campbell
www.karencampbellartist.com
Book Layout and Digital Design: KT Design, LLC
www.ktdesignllc.com

LET'S GET SOCIAL!

karencampbellartist.com

facebook.com/karencampbellartist

instagram.com/karencampbellartist

coolmamacrafts.etsy.com

youtube.com/coolmamacraftsapex

awesomeartschool.com

TABLE OF CONTENTS

WHAT PAGE CAN I FIND IT?

ADDITIONAL
RESOURCES

COLORED PENCILS, CRAYONS AND MARKERS ARE ALL AFFORDABLE COLORING OPTIONS AND OFTEN COME IN PORTRAIT PACKS WHICH HELPS MAKE CHOOSING SKIN TONES SO MUCH EASIER. IF YOU'D LIKE TO LEARN THE EXACT TECHNIQUES I USE TO CREATE AND COLOR THE FACES YOU SEE IN MY BOOKS, CHECK OUT MY ONLINE CLASSES WHICH ACCOMPANY MY ENTIRE HOW-TO-DRAW SERIES.

HOW TO DRAW FUN, FAB FACES:
Drawing fabulous front-facing female faces.

THE ART OF COLORING FACES WITH MARKER:
How to draw, color, blend and shade (both light and dark skin tones) with alcohol markers.

HOW TO DRAW MORE FUN, FAB FACES:
Drawing the female face in 3/4 view and profile.

HOW TO DRAW FUN, FAB FELLAS:
Drawing handsome guys from the front, 3/4 view and profile.

PLUS FIND FREE TUTORIALS AND REAL-TIME, DOWNLOADABLE CLASSES ON ACRYLICS, WATERCOLORS, ENCAUSTICS, MIXED MEDIA, ART JOURNALING AND MORE!

AWESOMEARTSCHOOL.COM

WELCOME

WELCOME TO YOUR PERSONAL GUIDE TO DRAWING FACES!
AS A MULTI-MEDIA ARTIST I HAVE ENJOYED DRAWING AND PAINTING
EVERYTHING FROM LANDSCAPES TO FLOWERS TO
AIRPLANES AND BOATS! BUT I WAS ALWAYS <u>SO</u> SUPER AFRAID TO
DRAW A PERSON, AND ESPECIALLY, A FACE!

YEEK!

THIS IS ABOUT ALL I COULD MUSTER!

BUT ONCE I TOOK AN INTRODUCTORY CLASS OR TWO
THAT BROKE DOWN ALL THE COMPLICATED PARTS INTO BASIC
STEP-BY-STEP SHAPES AND PATTERNS, I REALIZED IT WASN'T
SO HARD AFTER ALL!

AND ONCE YOU KNOW AND PRACTICE THE BASICS, OVER AND OVER,
THEN THE FUN WITH MAKING FACES <u>REALLY</u> BEGINS!

SO LET'S GET TO IT!

-KAREN

FIRST!

DRAW AN
OVAL!

AS YOU CAN SEE,
SOMETIMES THIS
TAKES MANY
TRIES THAT'S
OK! NO NEED
TO ERASE YET!

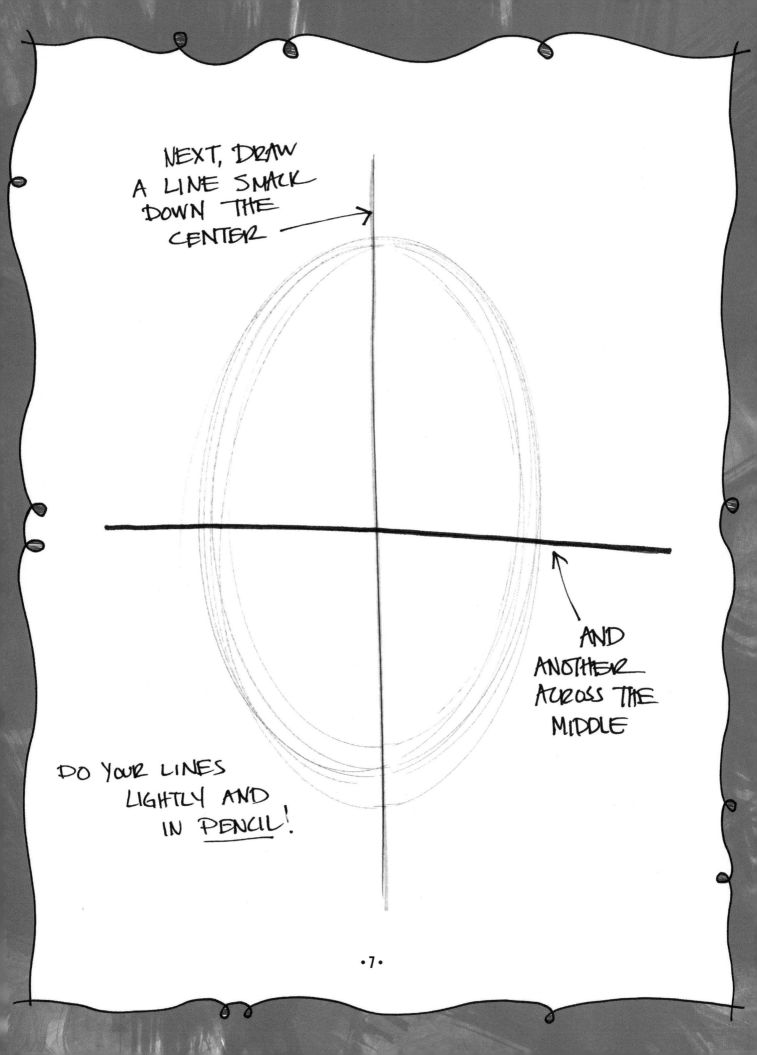

NEXT, DRAW A LINE SMACK DOWN THE CENTER

AND ANOTHER ACROSS THE MIDDLE

DO YOUR LINES LIGHTLY AND IN PENCIL!

NO NEED TO BE PERFECT!
I HAVEN'T ERASED YET,
HAVE YOU?
IT'S OKAY
TO LEAVE
EXTRA
MARKS
HERE &
THERE.

CHIN

NOW ADD
ANOTHER LIGHT
LINE BETWEEN
THE 1ST LINE ACROSS
AND THE CHIN

CAN YOU GUESS WHERE THE EYES, NOSE, AND MOUTH ARE GOING TO GO?

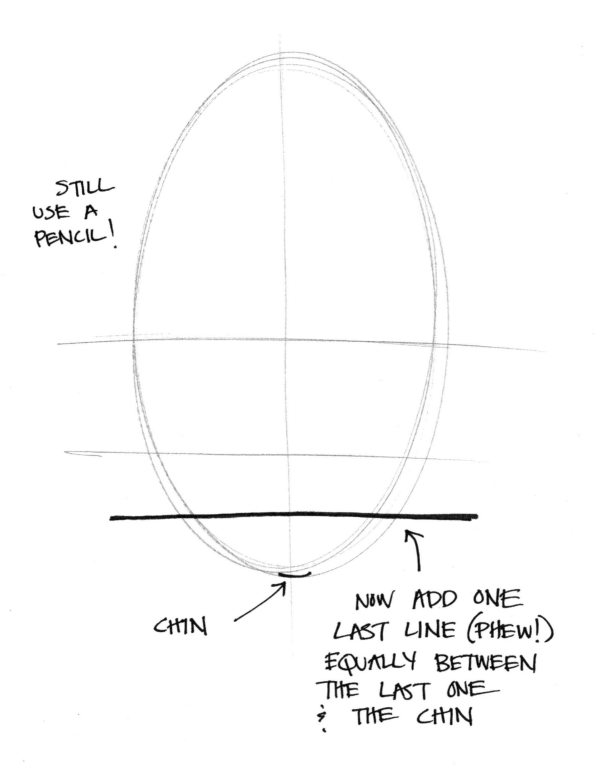

STILL USE A PENCIL!

CHIN

NOW ADD ONE LAST LINE (PHEW!) EQUALLY BETWEEN THE LAST ONE & THE CHIN

EEEK! THIS PAGE IS CREEPY, ISN'T IT? THESE FUNNY OVALS AND CIRCLES AS YOU SEE THEM HERE ARE PLACEHOLDERS FOR THE...

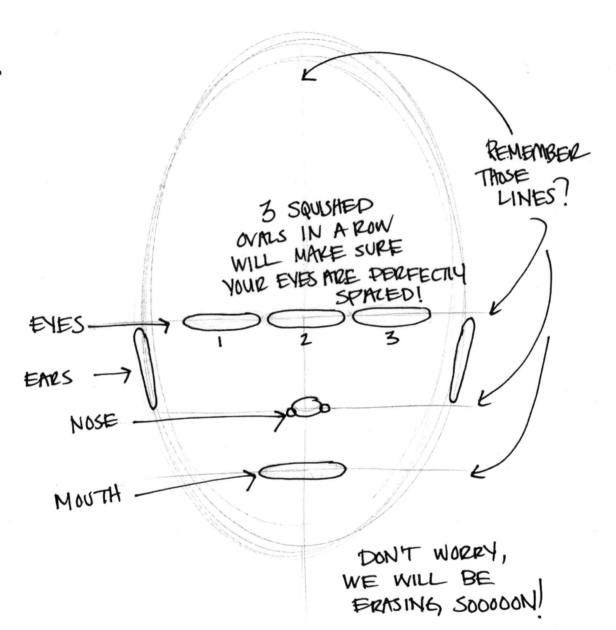

REMEMBER THOSE LINES?

3 SQUSHED OVALS IN A ROW WILL MAKE SURE YOUR EYES ARE PERFECTLY SPACED!

EYES

EARS

NOSE

MOUTH

1   2   3

DON'T WORRY, WE WILL BE ERASING SOOOOON!

HOLD ON TO THIS PAGE- WE WILL BE BACK TO THIS LATER!!!

THIS TIME I WILL GIVE YOU A HAND (YOU'RE WELCOME!). HERE'S MY OVAL AND ALL MY LINES. CAN YOU LIGHTLY SKETCH IN THE "3 EYES" (THE MIDDLE WILL BE ERASED LATER), NOSE, EARS, AND MOUTH IN THE RIGHT PLACES?

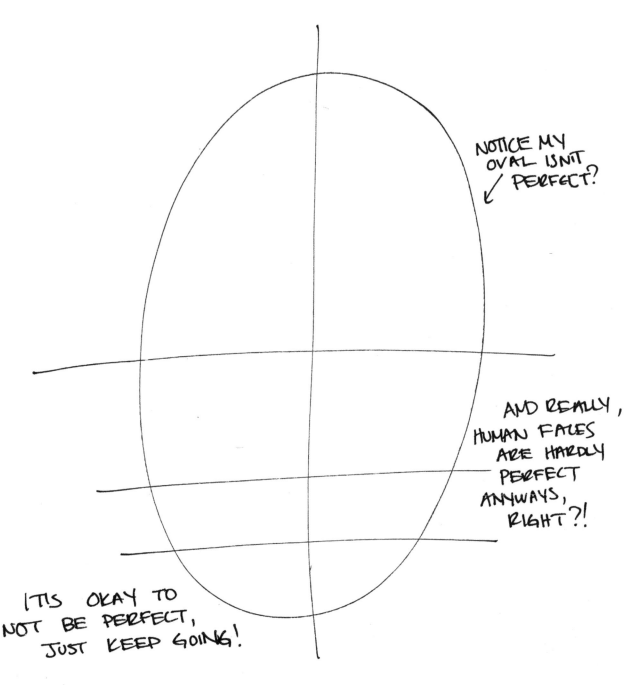

NOTICE MY OVAL ISN'T PERFECT?

AND REALLY, HUMAN FACES ARE HARDLY PERFECT ANYWAYS, RIGHT?!

IT'S OKAY TO NOT BE PERFECT, JUST KEEP GOING!

SO THE POINT OF ALL THAT LINE MAKING CRAZINESS IS THAT ONCE WE KNOW THE RIGHT SPOTS ON THE FACE, WE CAN START TO DRAW THEM ON FOR REAL.

SEE HOW MY LIGHT LINES HELP PUT ALL THE FEATURES IN THEIR RIGHT PLACES?

DARK

ONCE YOU HAVE DARKENED THE LINES YOU WANT TO KEEP, ERASE THE REST!

ADD A NECK!

WHEN YOU'RE DONE, GO BACK AND ERASE THOSE LIGHT LINES AND VOILÀ! YOU'VE GOT AN ACCURATELY DRAWN FACE!

NOW THAT WE HAVE THE RIGHT PLACES FOR OUR EYES, EARS, NOSE, AND MOUTH, WE CAN CREATE EACH ONE SEPARATELY AND GO BACK AND BUILD OUR BEAUTIFUL FACE!

LET'S BEGIN WITH EYES...

EYES

SQUISHED OVALS ARE A GOOD START!

POINT!

END IN A POINT

TEAR DUCTY-THINGYS
(ALSO POINTS)

NO ~~EYEBALLS~~ YET... LET'S PRACTICE THIS FIRST!

(THE POSSIBILITIES ARE ENDLESS!)

PRACTICE, PRACTICE, PRACTICE!

SEE? EVEN I AM MESSY. LEAVE IT!

MAKE ENDS COME TO-GETHER LIKE THIS

SEE HOW I LEFT MY MISTAKES? IT'S OK! WE ARE STILL JUST PRACTICING!

NOT BIG AND ROUND

TEAR DUCT POINTY THINGS MAKE YOUR EYES LOOK MORE REALISTIC!

EYELIDS ADD <u>TONS</u> OF PERSONALITY TO AN EYE.
SO LET'S SEE WHAT DIFFERENT SIZES WE CAN COME UP WITH!

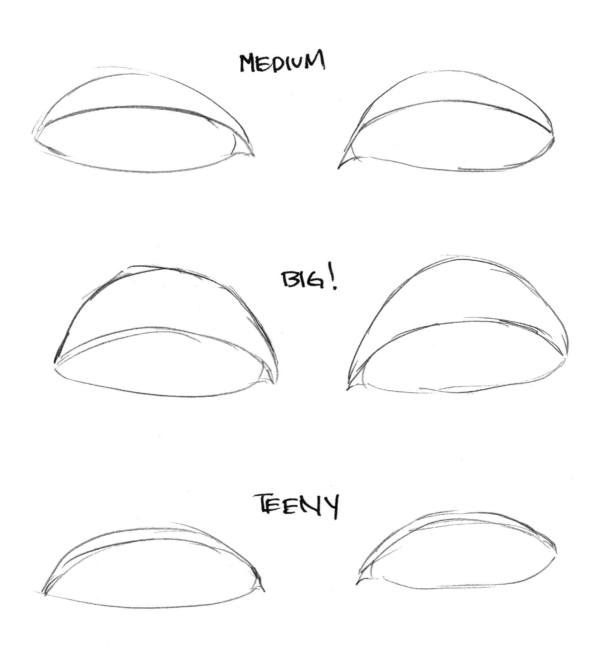

MEDIUM

BIG!

TEENY

WHEN COLORING EYELIDS, KEEP THE CENTERS WHITE, IT WILL MAKE THE EYE LOOK ROUNDED AND DRAMATIC! BRIGHT COLORS MAKE FOR AWESOME MAKE-UP EFFECTS!

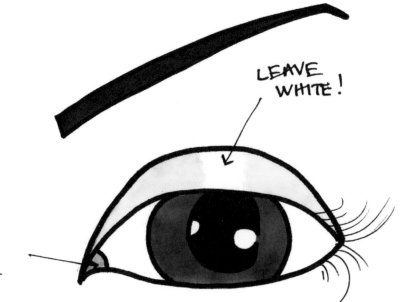

LEAVE WHITE!

ALWAYS ADD A TOUCH OF PINK TO TEAR DUCT!

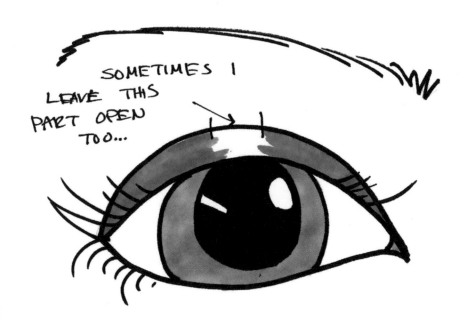

SOMETIMES I LEAVE THIS PART OPEN TOO...

MORE ON EYESHINE, LASHES AND BROWS COMING UP!

HERE'S AN EXAMPLE OF HOW I MIGHT DRAW AND COLOR A PAIR OF EYES. NOTE HER FANCY LIDS!

NOW IT'S YOUR TURN TO COLOR. GO ON!
MAKE THOSE EYES POP WITH SOME COOL MAKE-UP COLOR!

NOW IT'S FINALLY EYEBALL TIME!
THE NO. 1 RULE IS TO MAKE SURE YOU CHOP YOUR IRIS CIRCLE OFF AT THE TOP AND BOTTOM. WHAT IS THE IRIS??

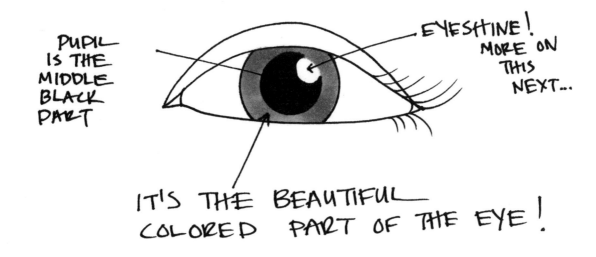

PUPIL IS THE MIDDLE BLACK PART

EYESHINE! MORE ON THIS NEXT...

IT'S THE BEAUTIFUL COLORED PART OF THE EYE!

AND WHEN YOU DRAW THE IRIS, YOU NEED TO MAKE SURE YOU DON'T SEE THE WHOLE THING (OR CIRCLE).

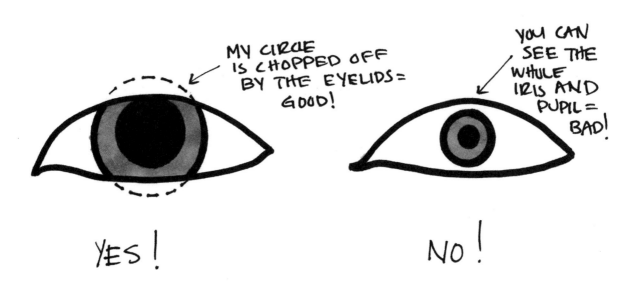

MY CIRCLE IS CHOPPED OFF BY THE EYELIDS = GOOD!

YOU CAN SEE THE WHOLE IRIS AND PUPIL = BAD!

YES!

NO!

EYE SHINE IS <u>CRUCIAL!</u>
DON'T FORGET TO LEAVE A LITTLE ROOM FOR SPARKLE WHEN YOU MAKE YOUR EYES!

IF USING MARKER, YOU MUST PLAN AHEAD!

MAKE SURE THEY MATCH!

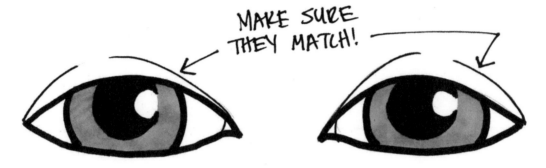

LEAVE A CIRCLE OPEN IN YOUR PUPILS AND FILL IN BLACK AROUND.

IF USING PENCIL, YOU CAN COLOR IN THE PUPIL AND THEN <u>ERASE</u> THE CIRCLE OR STREAKS TO MAKE THE EYESHINE.

ANOTHER WAY TO ADD EYESHINE TO YOUR CRAYON
OR COLORED PENCIL DRAWINGS IS TO ADD IT WITH
A WHITE MARKER. REMEMBER, THIS IS ART, BE
IMAGINATIVE AND HAVE FUN!

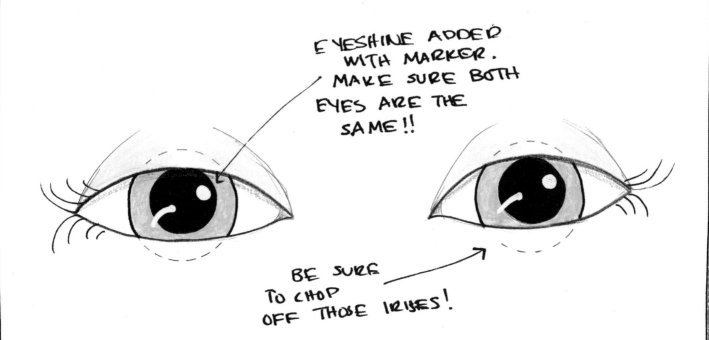

EYESHINE ADDED
WITH MARKER.
MAKE SURE BOTH
EYES ARE THE
SAME !!

BE SURE
TO CHOP
OFF THOSE IRISES!

IT'S FUN TO MIX YOUR MATERIALS WHEN MAKING ART.
TRY DRAWING FIRST IN PENCIL, OUTLINING IN PEN, AND
THEN COLORING IN WITH COLORED PENCIL!

A WORD ABOUT EYELASHES...
IT IS IMPORTANT TO NOTE THE DIRECTION THEY GROW...

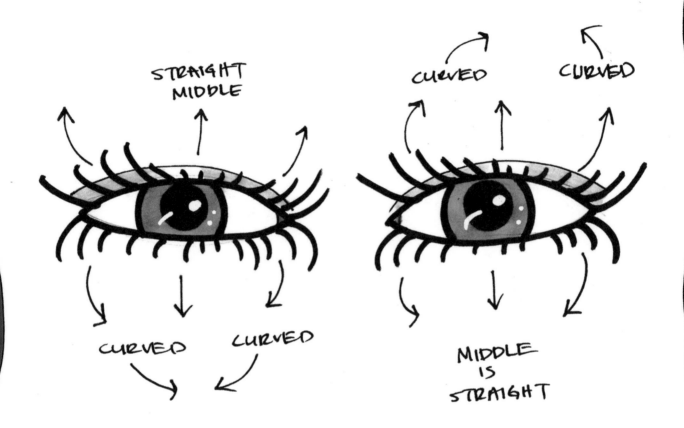

STRAIGHT MIDDLE

CURVED CURVED

CURVED CURVED

CURVED CURVED

MIDDLE IS STRAIGHT

YOU DON'T <u>HAVE</u> TO HAVE A MILLION LASHES
(THO YOU CAN!). SOMETIMES JUST A FEW IS LOVELY.

EYELASHES ARE FUN, LET'S MAKE SOME MORE.
FIRST ME, THEN YOU!

REAL
EYELASHES ARE
ALL DIFFERENT
LENGTHS SO
DON'T WORRY IF
YOURS ARE TOO!

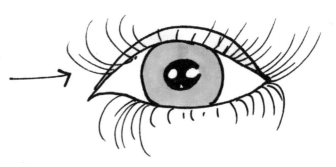

GIVE THEM A MATCH OR DRAW NEW EYES!

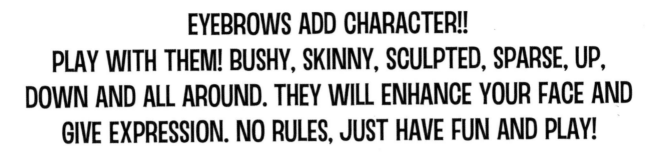

EYEBROWS ADD CHARACTER!!
PLAY WITH THEM! BUSHY, SKINNY, SCULPTED, SPARSE, UP,
DOWN AND ALL AROUND. THEY WILL ENHANCE YOUR FACE AND
GIVE EXPRESSION. NO RULES, JUST HAVE FUN AND PLAY!

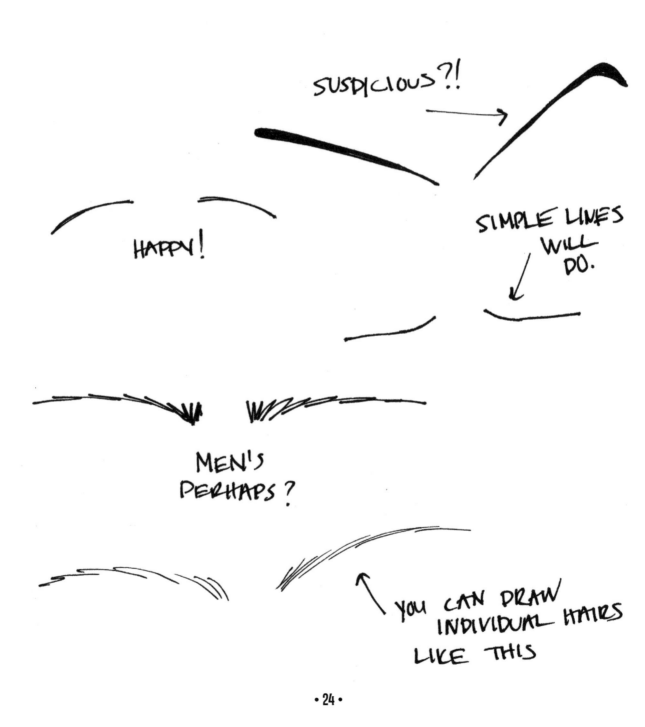

PLEASE HELP!
SHE NEEDS SOME PRETTY
BROWS AND LASHES!

NOW LET'S PRACTICE PUTTING IT ALL TOGETHER!

 EYESHAPE & EYELID

 IRIS (CHOP IT!)

 PUPIL

 EYESHINE

 EYELASHES & BROWS!

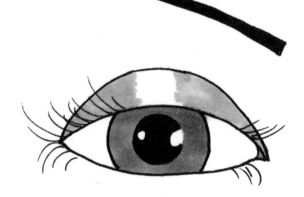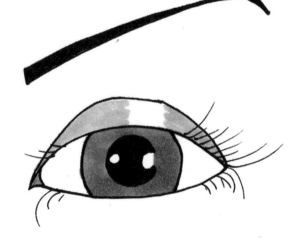

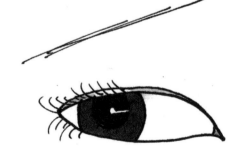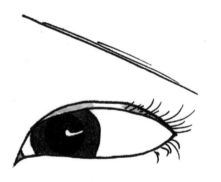

USE THE NEXT PAGE FOR YOUR OWN!

GO FOR IT!
ADD IRISES, LASHES, LIDS, AND BROWS!
⭐ DON'T FORGET THE EYESHINE! ⭐

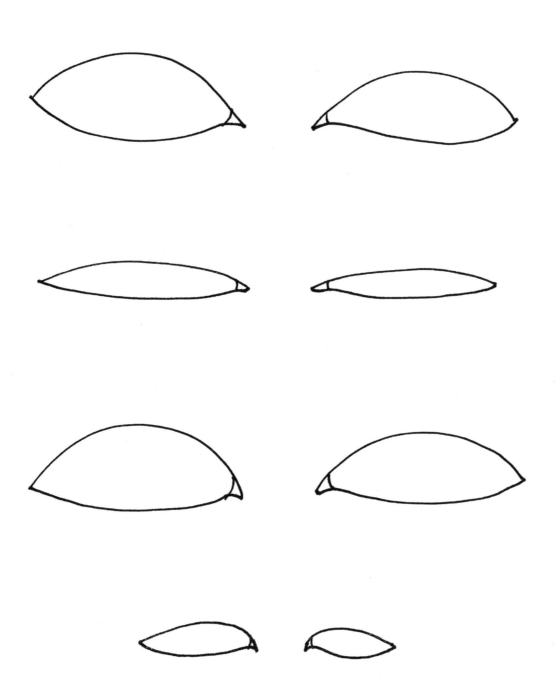

HELP! SHE CAN'T SEE!
GIVE HER SOME BEAUTIFUL EYES.

NOSES

NOW ONTO NOSES! WEIRD LOOKIN' THINGS BUT LUCKILY VERY EASY TO DRAW! HERE'S A COUPLE WAYS:

1. ( )   ADD PARENTHESES

2.   NEXT, SOME SQUASHED OVALS

3.   JOIN THEM UP, ADD A SWOOP

4.   AND THAT'S IT!

HERE'S ANOTHER VARIATION:

1.   ← DRAW THESE AS YOUR "PLACE HOLDERS"

2.   DARKEN THE IMPORTANT PARTS

3.   ← THE LINE UP FROM THE NOSE IS THE BRIDGE. IT IS OPTIONAL.

NOSES, LIKE ALL DRAWN FACIAL FEATURES, REALLY COME
TO LIFE WHEN YOU ADD SHADING TO YOUR DRAWINGS...
HERE'S A QUICK EXAMPLE:

LEAVING THE
NOSE BRIDGE
WHITE OR LIGHT
REALLY MAKES
THE FACE POP...

...AS DOES
ADDING SHADE
ON EITHER SIDE
OF THE NOSE,
AS WELL AS
UNDER

SEE HOW THE BRIDGE OF THE NOSE IS CREATED BY THE
SHADOWS AROUND THE EYES?

THANKS TO YOUR GUIDELINES, YOUR NOSE KNOWS EXACTLY WHERE TO GO!

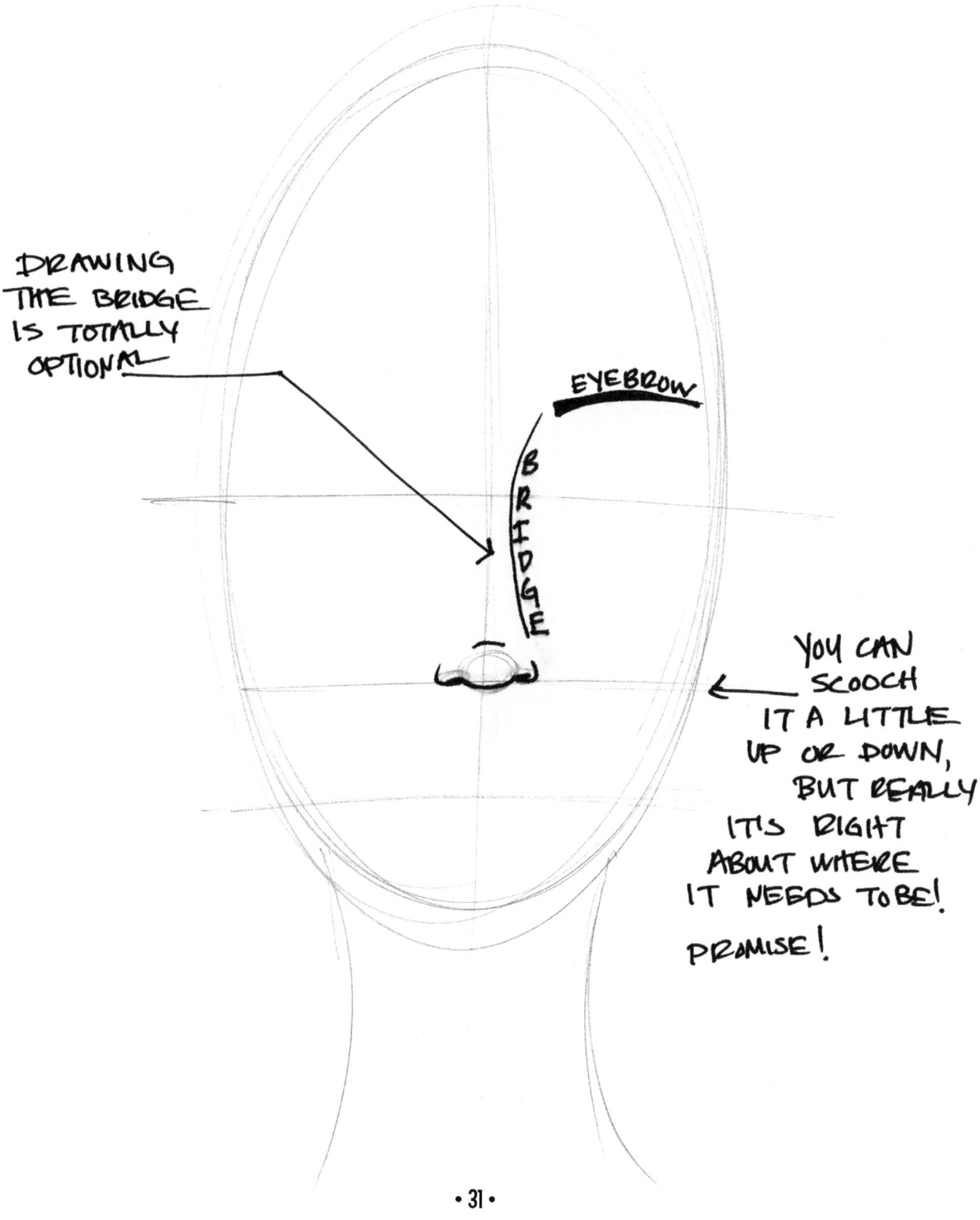

DRAWING THE BRIDGE IS TOTALLY OPTIONAL

EYEBROW

B R I D G E

YOU CAN SCOOCH IT A LITTLE UP OR DOWN, BUT REALLY IT'S RIGHT ABOUT WHERE IT NEEDS TO BE!

PROMISE!

HERE'S SOME MORE WAYS TO DRAW YOUR NOSE IN COLOR.

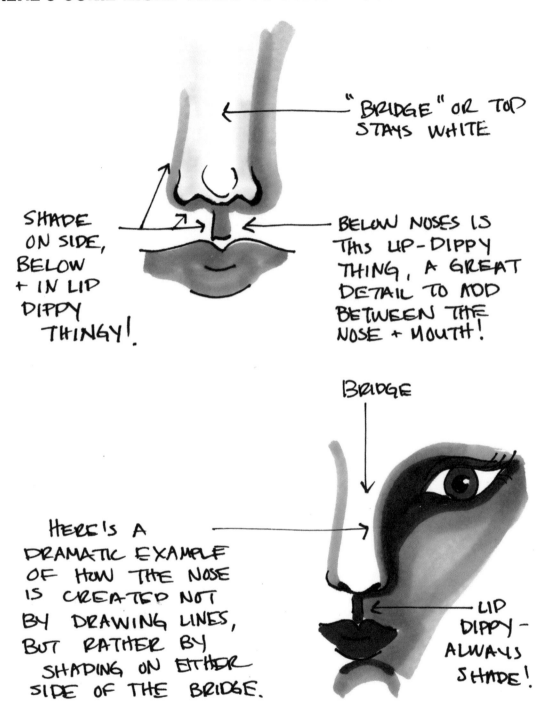

"BRIDGE" OR TOP STAYS WHITE

SHADE ON SIDE, BELOW + IN LIP DIPPY THINGY!

BELOW NOSES IS THIS LIP-DIPPY THING, A GREAT DETAIL TO ADD BETWEEN THE NOSE + MOUTH!

BRIDGE

HERE'S A DRAMATIC EXAMPLE OF HOW THE NOSE IS CREATED NOT BY DRAWING LINES, BUT RATHER BY SHADING ON EITHER SIDE OF THE BRIDGE.

LIP DIPPY — ALWAYS SHADE!

DON'T FORGET TO USE YOUR PENCIL GUIDELINES TO MAKE SURE YOUR NOSE KNOWS RIGHT WHERE TO GO!

SOME ARTISTS DRAW THE BRIDGE, OR PART OF THE BRIDGE. OFTEN IT LEADS INTO THE EYEBROW LIKE THIS.

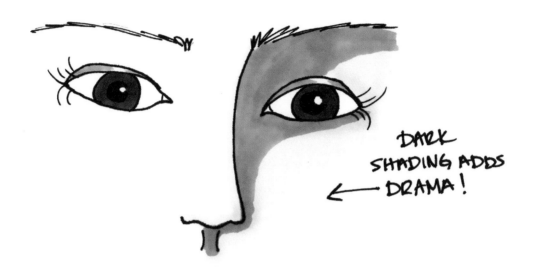

DARK SHADING ADDS ← DRAMA!

YOU COULD ALSO DRAW JUST A PARTIAL BRIDGE.

THE "BROKEN" BRIDGE LINE IS QUITE LOVELY. →

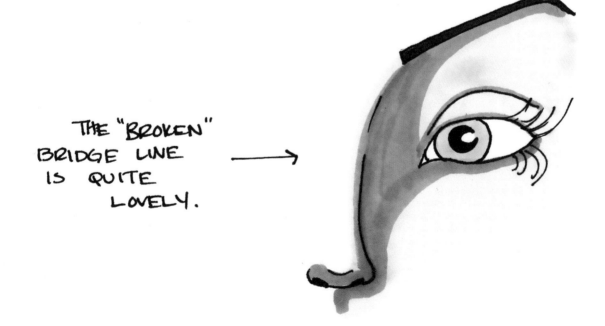

HELP! SHE CAN'T SMELL THE FLOWER IN HER HAIR! TRY GIVING HER A SIMPLE NOSE.

LIPS

LUCKY LIPS ARE NEXT!
SUPER EASY AND FUN, LET'S GO!

1.

2.

3.

4.

5.

6. 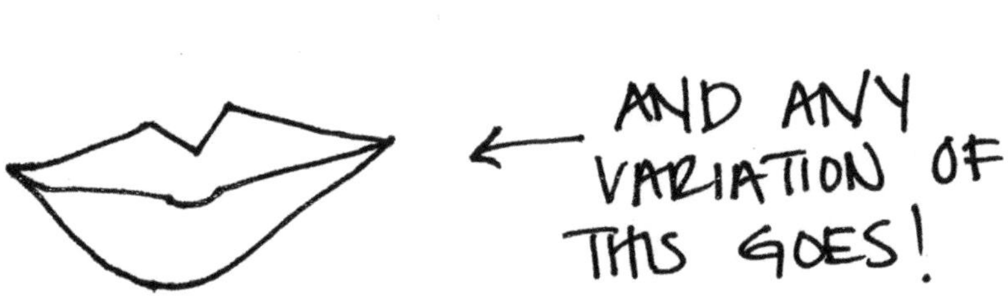 ← AND ANY VARIATION OF THIS GOES!

LIPS ARE SUPER FUN TO DRAW!

LIP-TASTIC!

SMOOCHES!

REMEMBER TO ALWAYS USE YOUR GUIDELINES TO PLACE YOUR FEATURES.

IF YOUR HEAD OVAL APPEARS TOO TALL AFTER YOU PLACE YOUR FEATURES, SIMPLY TRIM IT OFF A BIT.

YOU HAVE SOME MORE WIGGLE ROOM UP OR DOWN THAN THE OTHER FEATURES OF THE FACE.

TRY MOVING IT TO SEE WHAT HAPPENS!

THIS DOWNWARD LINE PRODUCES THE APPEARANCE OF A MORE DUTINCT CHIN. IT, TOO, IS OPTIONAL.

CHIN

YOU CAN ALSO LOWER THE BOTTOM CHIN LINE TO MAKE MORE ROOM FOR THE MOUTH.

EARS

AS FAR AS EARS GO, I TRY TO AVOID THEM BUT SOMETIMES IT'S SUPER FUN TO DRAW IN COOL EARRINGS SO IT'S GOOD TO KNOW THEIR BASIC FORM!

KEEP IT SIMPLE!

LET THE JEWELRY BE THE STAR OF THE SHOW!

TUCK HAIR BEHIND IF YOU LIKE!
AGAIN, SIMPLE IS STILL BEST.

HMMM... HOW MANY DIFFERENT EARRING DESIGNS CAN WE COME UP WITH? HERE'S A FEW. COLOR THEM IN! BET YOU CAN COME UP WITH A WHOLE LOT MORE. GO FOR IT!

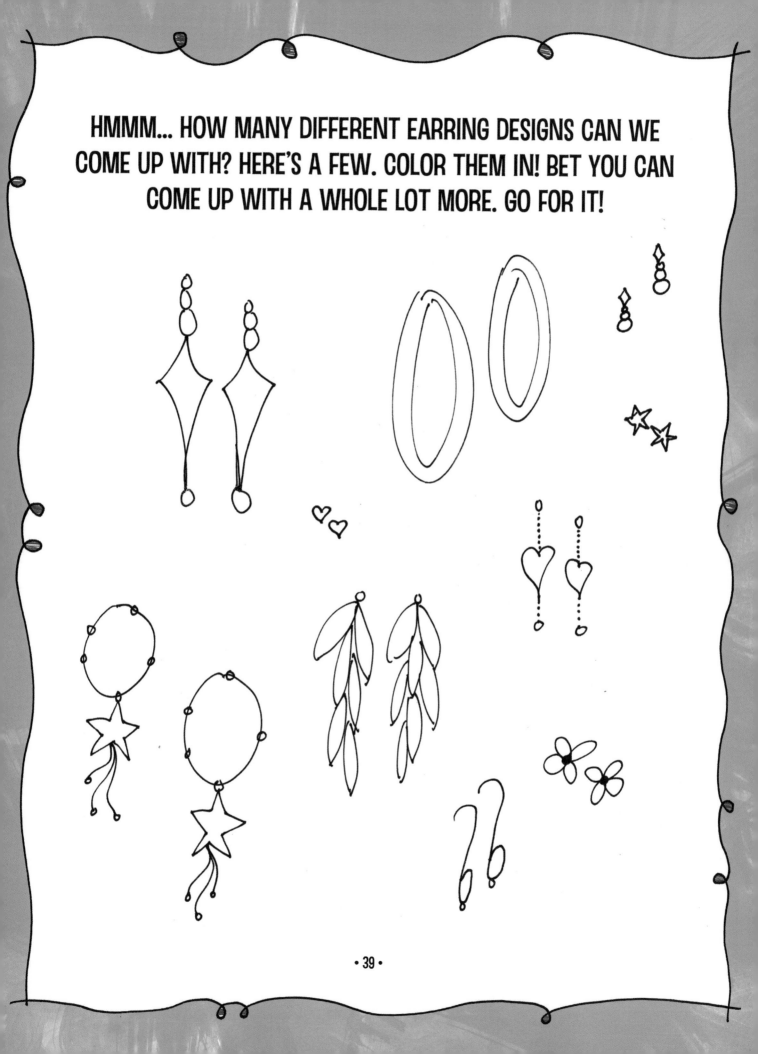

THIS LOVELY LADY JUST BOUGHT NEW EARRINGS TO MATCH HER NECKLACE. DRAW AND COLOR THEM IN!

THE EARS SNUGGLE IN PERFECTLY BETWEEN THE GUIDELINES FOR THE EYES AND NOSE. WHILE THIS IS NOT ANATOMICALLY ACCURATE, FOR OUR DRAWING PURPOSES, IT WORKS OUT JUST FINE!

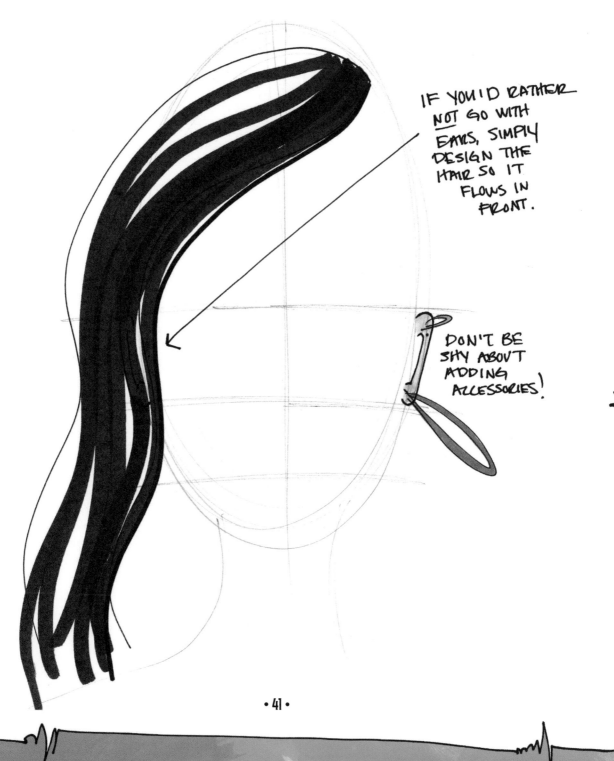

IF YOU'D RATHER NOT GO WITH EARS, SIMPLY DESIGN THE HAIR SO IT FLOWS IN FRONT.

DON'T BE SHY ABOUT ADDING ACCESSORIES!

HAIR

AAAAAH! WE ALMOST FORGOT TO DRAW THE HAIR!
AND THAT'S THE BEST PART (GET IT? <u>PART</u>?).

<u>THREE</u> THINGS YOU NEED TO DO:

<u>FIRST</u>: PICK A PART NEAR THE TOP.
<u>SECOND</u>: HAIR GOES DOWN ACROSS THE FOREHEAD LINE.
<u>THIRD</u>: HAIR ALSO GROWS UP AND OVER THE OVAL WE DREW FOR THE FACE.

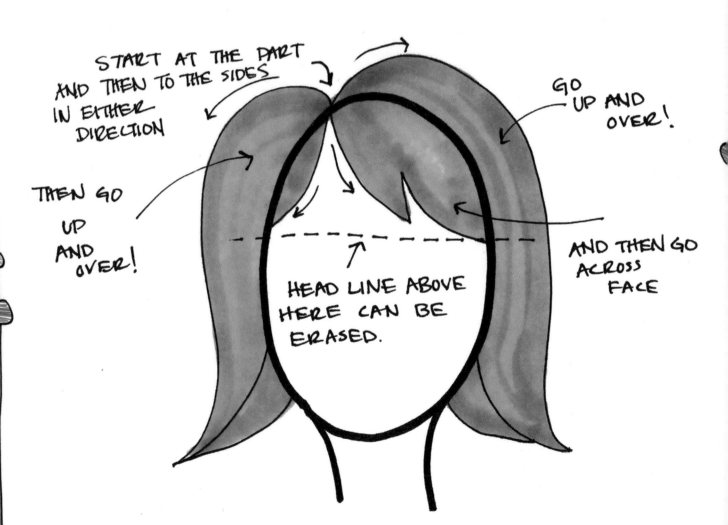

I'LL MAKE UP SOME HAIRSTYLES...
THE DOTTED LINE IS WHERE THE OVAL WAS, REMEMBER?

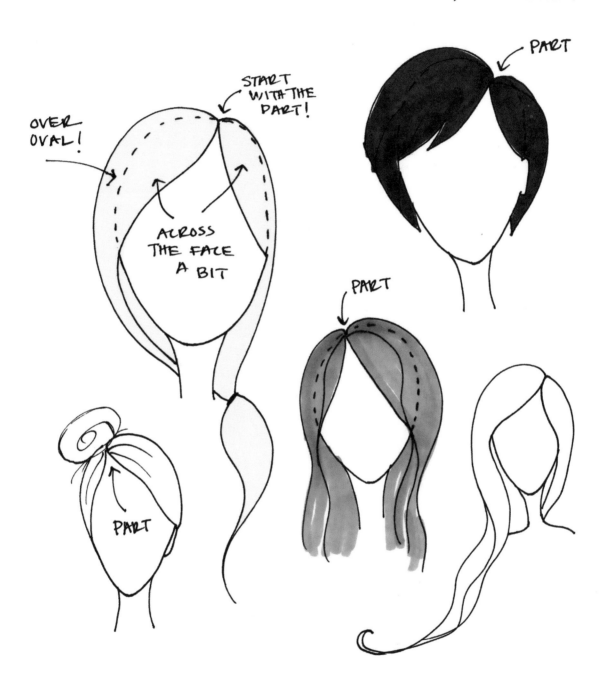

OH MAN, LOOKS LIKE I FORGOT TO COLOR SOME. CAN YOU HELP ME OUT PLEASE?

HERE'S SOME MORE TO TRY...

SHORT BOB

HIGH-PONY

PIGS

HEAD BAND

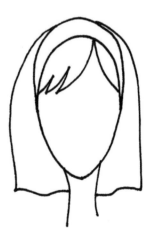

CURLY

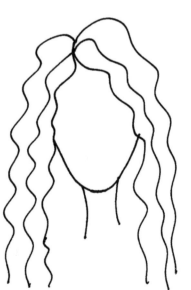

DON'T FORGET TO BE CREATIVE!
WHO SAYS HAIR HAS TO BE BLONDE, BROWN, RED, OR BLACK?!

LET'S PRACTICE OUR CREATIVITY!
GIVE THIS GIRL SOME CRAZY COLORS!

BE BRAVE! TRY A BRAID...

OR A BOW!

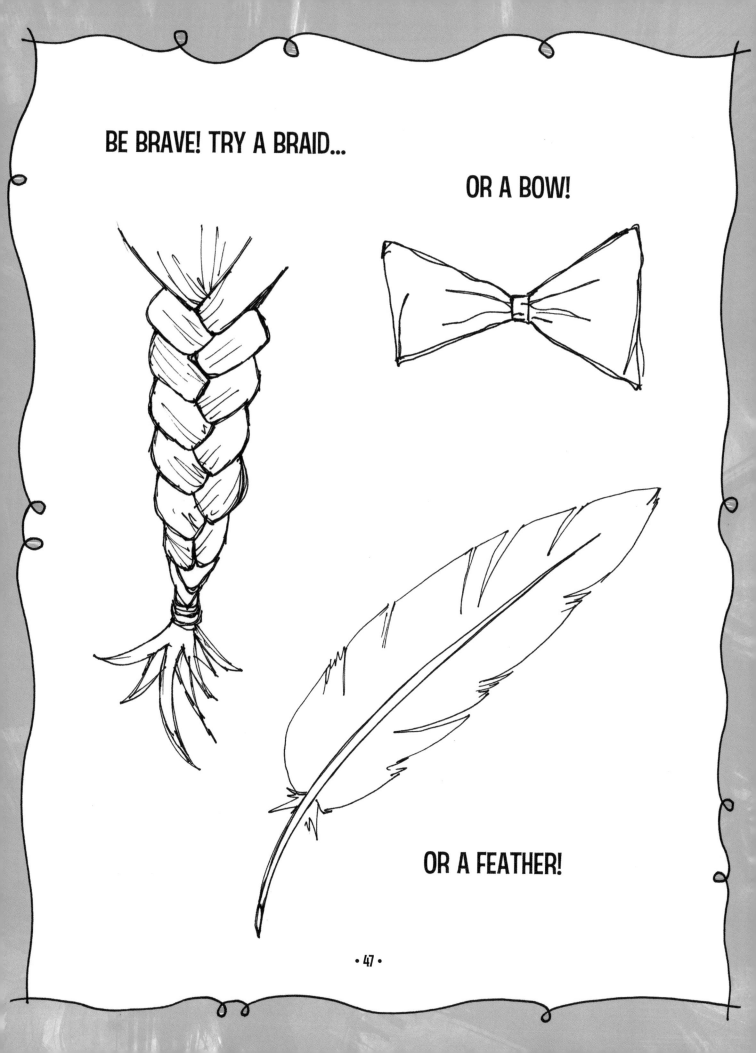

OR A FEATHER!

FACES

I'M GOING TO PUT ALL THE PIECES TOGETHER AND DRAW SOME FACES FOR YOU TO COLOR. AFTER THAT I WANT <u>YOU</u> TO GO GRAB SOME BLANK SHEETS AND START MAKING YOUR OWN!

USE LOTS OF COLOR...

DON'T BE AFRAID TO GET SILLY!

TRY NEW THINGS!

TRY VARYING YOUR FEATURES WHEN YOU START GETTING COMFORTABLE. MAKE BIGGER EYES, TRY A FACE WITH A TINY MOUTH. EXPERIMENT, PLAY, SEE WHAT HAPPENS AND HAVE FUN!

TRY NOT TO CARE TOO MUCH ABOUT WHAT YOU ARE DRAWING. JUST RELAX AND POP IN THOSE FEATURES (USE YOUR LINES THO!). YOU MAY JUST BE SURPRISED BY WHO SHOWS UP ON YOUR PAGE!

SO NOW THAT WE ARE AWESOME FACE DRAWERS, (COME ON! ADMIT IT, WE ARE!), WE NEED TO HAVE A LITTLE CHAT ABOUT SHADING. NOTHING MAJOR, BUT EVEN JUST A LITTLE CAN MAKE YOUR DRAWING GO A LONG WAY, OKAY?

BASICALLY, PARTS OF YOUR FACE THAT STICK OUT ARE THE LIGHTEST AND THE PLACES THAT GO "BACK" ARE THE DARKEST.

GO GRAB A MIRROR AND YOU'LL SEE JUST WHAT I MEAN.
(SERIOUSLY! GO GET ONE OR GET IN FRONT OF ONE!)
WHAT STICKS OUT?

- THE NOSE
- THE FOREHEAD
- THE CHIN

SIMPLE!

AND LOOK AGAIN NOW... WHAT PLACES GO WAY BACK
OR IN TOWARDS YOUR HEAD?

- AROUND THE EYES.
- AROUND THE FACE.
- AROUND THE NOSE.
- THE NECK.

SOUNDS LIKE PLENTY TO ME, NOW LET'S GET SHADING
SO YOU CAN REALLY SEE.

I'LL DO A DRAWING IN MARKER TO SHOW YOU WHERE
TO PUT DOWN DARKER SHADES AND WHERE TO LEAVE IT
THE LIGHTEST, OK? HAVING 3 TONES TO EVERY DRAWING
ADDS SO SO MUCH DEPTH AND DIMENSION.

NOSE, FOREHEAD
AND CHIN STAY
LIGHT OR
WHITE!

PUT SHADE
UNDER ANY
HAIR FALL-
ING ON THE
FACE

ALL
AROUND
THE FACE
OUTLINE
IF YOU
LIKE!

UNDER
NOSE
AND
MOUTH!

YOU CAN
SHADE JUST
ONE SIDE
OF THE NOSE
OR BOTH!

ALWAYS PUT
SHADING UNDER
THE NECK

NOTE: SHADING IS TOTALLY OPTIONAL! IF IT'S TOO SCARY
OR TOO MUCH, SKIP IT! BUT AT LEAST GIVE IT A SHOT!

HERE'S ANOTHER SHADING EXAMPLE.
SEE HOW THE LOOK CHANGES DEPENDING ON WHERE YOU PUT THE DARKEST & LIGHTEST PARTS? OVERALL THO, THE BASIC PLACES REMAIN THE SAME.

ONE SIDED SHADING GIVES A STRONG IMPRESSION OF A LIGHT SOURCE COMING FROM SOMEWHERE.

A REALLY COOL EFFECT IS HAVING ALL OR MOST OF THE SHADING GO TO ONE SIDE.

DOESN'T THIS LOOK COOL?

KEEP THAT NOSE WHITE!

AND CHIN TOO...

HERE ARE SOME MORE SHADING EXAMPLES.
STILL STUCK? LOOK AT BLACK & WHITE PHOTOS ONLINE.

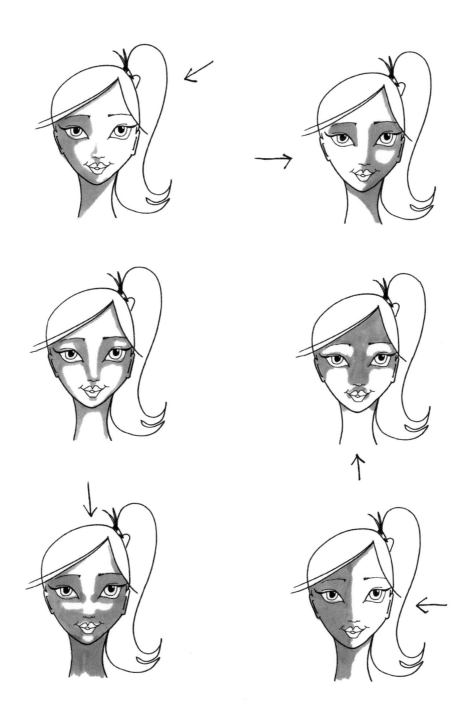

THE ARROW INDICATES WHERE THE LIGHT SOURCE IS COMING FROM!

WHEN SHADING DARKER SKIN TONES, THE SAME RULE OF 3 SHADES STILL APPLIES! THE OVERALL SHADES ARE SIMPLY DARKER.

HERE'S AN EXAMPLE OF SHADING WITH WATERCOLOR. WHAT IS YOUR FAVORITE MEDIUM TO CREATE IN?

YOU CAN ADD FURTHER BITS OF WHITE OR HIGHLIGHTS ON THE CHEEKS, EYEBROW BRIDGES AND EYELIDS

NOTICE THE HIGHLIGHTS OF WHITE ON HER NOSE, FOREHEAD & CHIN!

HERE IS A DRAWING I DID IN PENCIL.
SEE HOW THE SHADING IS STILL THE SAME? YOU CAN STILL
SEE 3 VARIATIONS, LIGHT, MEDIUM, AND DARK.

YOU CAN USE THE SAME SHADING PRINCIPLES WHEN YOU PAINT! DARKEST AREAS ARE SPOTS THAT RECEDE (GO BACK), WHILE AREAS THAT STICK OUT ARE LIGHTEST & BRIGHTEST.

NOW LET'S SEE YOU TRY SOME SHADING.
REMEMBER, THIS IS JUST FOR FUN!
IF IT DOESN'T WORK OUT, TRY AGAIN. DRAW ANOTHER AND
ANOTHER! EVERY TIME YOU TRY, IT SHARPENS UP THOSE
SKILLS AND YOU WILL ONLY GET BETTER AND BETTER.
PROMISE!!!

LAST ONE FOR NOW!
CAN YOU DO ME A FAVOR AND COLOR HER IN FOR ME?
THANKS. BE BRAVE! TRY ADDING SOME SHADING OR
COLOR IN SOME ROSEY CHEEKS!

NOW THAT YOU HAVE MASTERED ALL THE SKILLS YOU
NEED TO DRAW FACES INCLUDING THE:

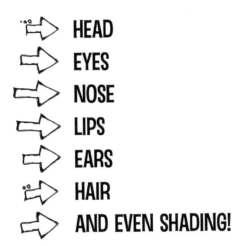

➡ HEAD
➡ EYES
➡ NOSE
➡ LIPS
➡ EARS
➡ HAIR
➡ AND EVEN SHADING!

YOU ARE READY TO GO FORTH INTO THE WORLD AND
PRACTICE YOUR OWN FACE! YES!
TAKE YOUR SKILLS AND HONE THEM. GET AN ART
JOURNAL, PLAY IN DIFFERENT MEDIUMS. HAVE FUN!

FIGURE OUT WHAT YOU LIKE TO USE BEST.
IS IT PENCIL? MARKERS? WATERCOLOR?
COLORED PENCIL? PAINT?

YOU CAN PRACTICE DRAWING AND PAINTING FACES IN
ANY MEDIUM. SO WHAT ARE YOU WAITING FOR?!

ABOUT THE AUTHOR

KAREN CAMPBELL

KAREN IS A FULL TIME ARTIST. SHE LIVES IN APEX, NC WITH HER SUPER SUPPORTIVE HUSBAND AND THREE TOTALLY AWESOME BOYS.

 See her portfolio, read her blog and shop original artwork and prints: www.karencampbellartist.com

 See videos of the artist at work! youtube.com/CoolMamaCraftsApex

CAN'T GET ENOUGH DRAWING AND PAINTING FUN?
CHECK OUT ALL OF KAREN'S ONLINE ART CLASSES AND FREE TUTORIALS AT:

AWESOMEARTSCHOOL.COM

BE SURE TO CHECK OUT THESE OTHER BOOKS BY THE AUTHOR:

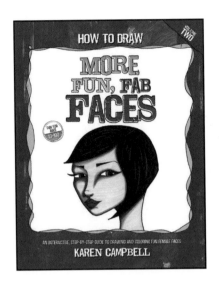

A STEP-BY-STEP GUIDE TO DRAWING THE FEMALE FACE IN 3/4 VIEW AND PROFILE.

A COMPREHENSIVE GUIDE TO DRAWING AND COLORING THE MALE FACE INCLUDING FRONT FACING, 3/4 VIEW AND PROFILE.

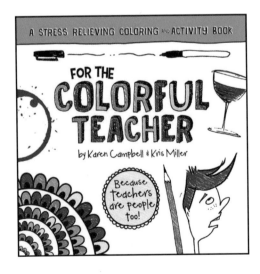

A LIGHT-HEARTED ACTIVITY AND COLORING BOOK FOR TEACHERS WITH A SENSE OF HUMOR. BECAUSE TEACHERS ARE PEOPLE TOO! MAKES THE PERFECT GIFT!

AVAILABLE EXCLUSIVELY ON AMAZON.

Printed in Great Britain
by Amazon